CW01651633

Ply Split Braiding

An introduction to Designs in Single Course Twining
by Julie Hedges

Ply Split Braiding
An introduction to Designs in Single Course Twining

By Julie Hedges

First edition published in 2006 by Julie Hedges Books

ISBN 13: 978-0-9554187-0-9

Second revised edition published by Julie Hedges Books in 2018

ISBN 13: 978-0-9554187-5-4

www.juliehedges.co.uk

Designed, edited and produced by Julie Hedges Books

Printed by Creative Digital Printing Solutions, Shrewsbury SY1 3TF
www.creativedigitalprinting.com

Dedication

To my mother Dorrie, who gave me the time and space to achieve this.

Acknowledgements

With Thanks to
Nick Hedges for continuing support and photographic and computer expertise;
Peter Collingwood, without whom ply-splitting would have remained a hidden art;
Ann Norman, for the use of diagrams 1, 3, 13 and 15;
Dr Ann Brammer for image of 'South China Seas' neckpiece;
Jennie Parry for editing and encouragement;
and all the students who have helped me to refine the designs.

Contents

A collection of the ply-split designs described in this book

Origins and recent developments
The technique
Getting starting with ply-split braids
About the designs

Overdressed camel at the Pushkar Camel Fair wearing a range of ply-split regalia

Julie ply-splitting with Ishwar Singh, camel girth maker. Photo by Joan Hitchcox.

Origins and recent developments

Ply-Split Braiding has been found extensively in Rajasthan and Gujarat, north-west India, where it has been used to make camel girths and animal regalia. During the 1980's, Peter Collingwood travelled to India many times and collected and analysed braided artefacts, the techniques of which had never been documented before. His researches culminated in a book 'The Techniques of Ply - Split Braiding' published in 1998. During this time lectures, workshops and demonstrations given by Peter in the UK, Europe and USA brought Ply-Splitting to a wider audience.
Consequently the technique has since been explored and developed in a number of directions. The traditional girths are made from goat hair yarn or sometimes cotton. Contemporary braidmakers also use cords made of a variety of yarns including , linen, hemp, silk, worsted, paper, or rayon.
Being an 'off loom' technique shapes may be made and combined to make more complex designs. Sections may be braided independently, brought together and divided at will to make net like structures. Finished pieces may vary in scale according to the size, quality & diameter of the cords used with potential from fine neckpieces, bracelets etc. to larger vessels and sculptural works.

Details of ply-split camel girths

My introduction to Ply-Splitting

After attending a workshop on Ply-Split Braiding, taught by Peter Collingwood in conjunction with the Animal Regalia exhibition held in 1989 at the Surrey Institute of Art & Design Farnham, UK, I became fascinated by the technique. Since then I have explored and developed the technique to make both functional and small sculptural pieces. Much of my work has been based on the Single Course Oblique Twining structure, see Glossary on page 45, and a selection of designs based on this method of Ply-Splitting are introduced in this book.

Ply-split neckpiece in linen, using Diagonal Stripe,Waves and Zigzag designs

Ply-Split belt, Oriental Waves design in linen

The Technique

Designing starts with the choice of yarn and this, as well as the cord-making process, determines the quality of the cords and subsequent feel and look of ply-split braids.
Ideally the yarn used should be smooth and non-hairy and this is made into highly twisted plied cords. These are commonly 4 ply cords, but 2 or 3 ply cords are sometimes used.

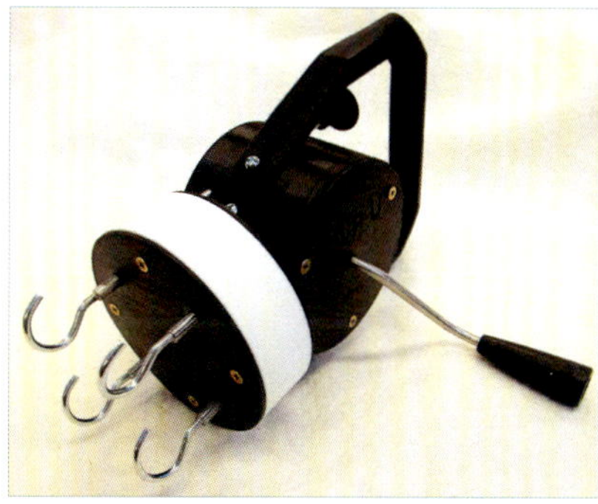

The Kipu 4 hook cordwinder

To make the 4 ply cords

Four elements of yarn of equal length are twisted separately under tension, putting on as much twist as possible without them snaring. (Initial Over Twist). These are then plied together under tension (Controlled Counter Twist) making highly twisted smooth cords. Many braiders use a 4 hooked cordwinder for this purpose. Two manual winders are shown opposite. Cords may be made up of single elements of one, two, three or four colours or multiple ends per element.
Once the cords are made, the ply-splitting process is very portable.
For more detailed information see Making Cords for use in Ply-Splitting on page 35.

The Apollo 4 hook cordwinder

Tools for splitting plies

Any two cords that cross can be split in one of two ways and it helps to have an efficient tool to assist in this. The two tools which are most often used are the gripfid and the latchet hook. These tools are used for splitting the cords and drawing a cord through the plies of one or more cords.

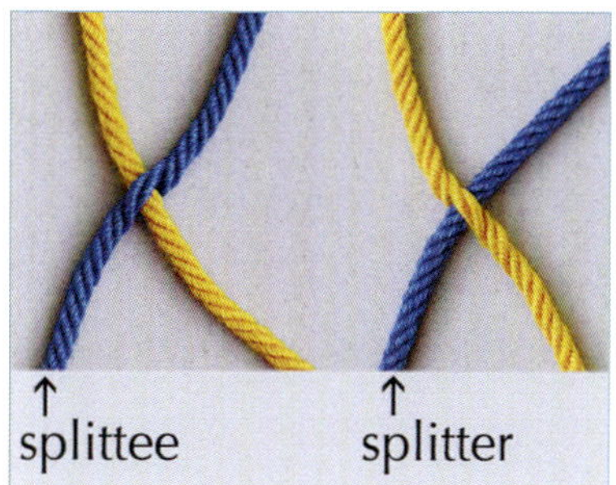

Any two cords that cross can be split in one of two ways

The Gripfid

Based on the Swedish fid, traditionally used for splicing rope, this tool was developed by the knot maker Stuart Grainger and is ideal for ply-splitting. A cord, the splittee, is easily split by the gripfid's point . The end of the splitter cord is placed in the taperered end of the tube which grips it. The splitter is then drawn back through the splittee before being released. Gripfids are available in various diameters and the tube size is chosen to match the diameter of cords in use. A 5 mm gripfidwas used for the samples in this book.

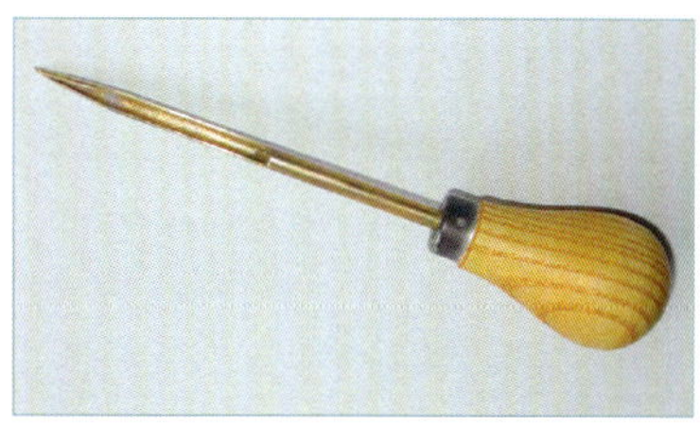

Gripfid

The Latchet Hook

A rug latchet hook or a long-shafted knitting machine latchet hook mounted into a handle may be used. The hook splits a cord, the splittee, in the closed position and another cord, the splitter is encircled by the closed hook and the looped end is drawn back through the splittee. The disadvantage of this tool is that it is harder to draw the doubled-over splitter through the splittee.

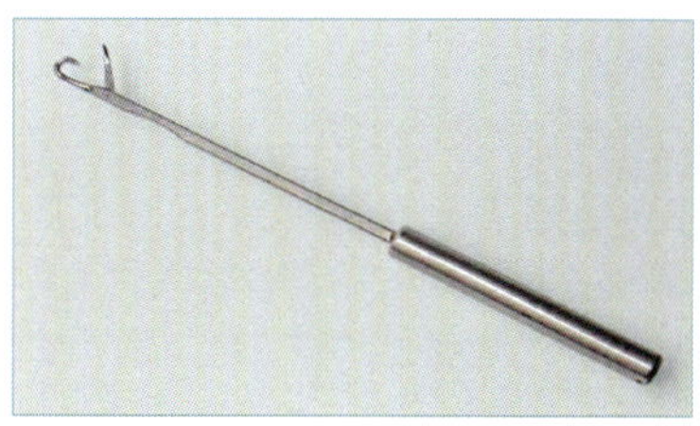

Latchet hook

Once the 4 ply braids are made there are two basic ply-split techniques from which most others are derived.

Ply-Split Darning

A weft thread or cord is passed through a series of 4 ply cords, the weft being taken through the ply of each cord with 2 ply above and 2 ply below, (2 ply ↑ and 2 ply ↓). The resulting band is made up of the series of vertical 4 ply cords intersected horizontally by the weft which travels through the sequence of cords from left to right and back.

This technique is covered in Ply-Split Braiding, Further Techniques by Julie Hedges.

Ply-split Darning

Ply-Split Braiding

A series of cords intersect each other in sequence, splitting the ply 2 above and 2 below, (2 ply ↑ and 2 ply ↓). The braid design depends on the colour order of the cords and the sequence in which the cords are split by each other.

There are two main methods of Ply-Split Braiding:

1 **Plain (oblique) Twining (PT): each cord alternately splits and is split by each successive cord it crosses.**
This technique is covered in Ply-Split Braiding, Further Techniques, Julie Hedges.

2 **Single Course (oblique) Twining (SCoT): a splitter cord passes through two or more successive cords that it crosses in sequence. This is the technique described in this book.**

Ply Split Braiding (SCoT)

Splitting the Plies

It is usual to split the cords with 2 ply ↑ and 2 ply ↓ leaving a quarter twist between the plies. i.e. with one new ply plus the adjacent previous ply, thus progressing down the cords on each row.
See Diagram 1.

If you are right handed, pick up the cord you wish to split (the splittee) with the thumb and first finger of your left hand and roll it against the twist to open up the plies before inserting the gripfid point or closed latchet hook, held in your right hand, between the plies.

If the cord is Z twisted you will roll it towards you, clockwise.

If the cord is S twisted you will roll it away from you, anticlockwise.

By picking up each splittee in turn in this way and inserting the gripfid or latchet hook you work across the row, counting the cords if necessary. The splitter is then placed in the gripfid or latchet hook and drawn back through the splittees. This will soon become an automatic manoeuvre.

It is usual for right-handers to pick up the cords in the left hand, insert the gripfid from the right and draw the splitter through from left to right. If you are left handed you will need to reverse the above procedure.

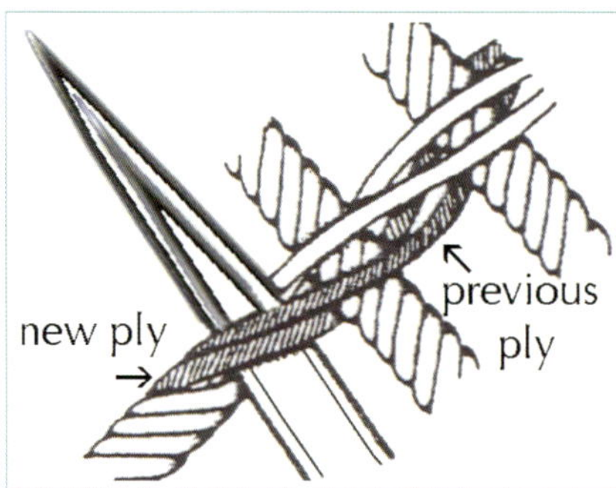

Diagram 1. 2 ply ↑ 2 ply ↓
leaving a quarter twist

Getting started with Ply Split Braids

Make 4 ply cords for use. See Making Cords for use in Ply-Splitting, page 35. It is essential that the cords are highly twisted and have smooth unknotted ends.

Starting on a kilt pin using a latchet hook

To prepare the cords for use:

Either cut the cords to the required length and seal by rolling them between the fingers with PVA glue or bind with transparent sticky tape at the required length and cut.

There are several methods of starting a ply-split braid and a few are described below.

a **Starting on a rod, kilt pin etc.**

b **Starting with single cords**

c **Starting on a buckle or ring**

d **A single loop start.**

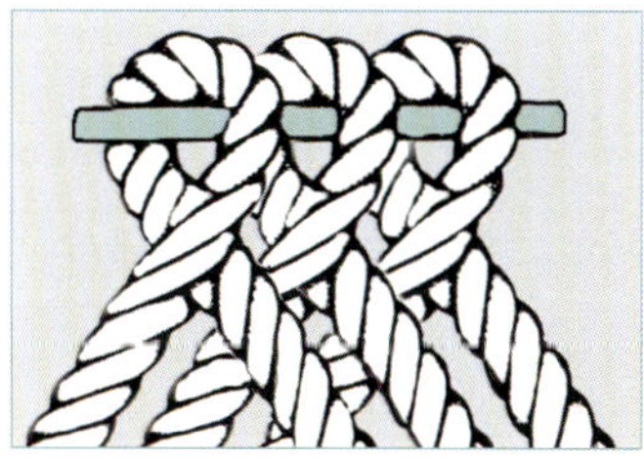

Diagram 2. Starting on a rod

a Starting on a rod, kilt pin etc.

- Prepare a set of highly twisted 4 ply cords.
- Take a cord and fold it in half to find the centre point.
- Take one end of the cord through itself just below the centre point, by splitting the cord 2 ply ↑ and 2 ply ↓ to form a loop. Place this looped cord over the rod and tighten.
- Take the other cords in turn and repeat, making sure that they are all mounted on the rod with the cords coming from the loops in the same direction. See Diagram 2

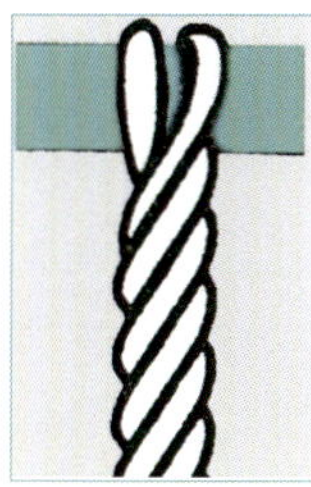

Diagram 3. Starting with a single cord

b Starting with single cords

- If a single cord is required for a particular number or colour sequence then if possible use a cord made with one uncut end, 'Eye' ' See Terms used in making cords making on page 44. This cord may either be passed through itself to make a loop, or the Eye may be mounted directly onto a rod or another cord after which the safety tie may be discarded. See Diagram 3.
- If a single cord with two cut ends is used, make the loop about 6 cm from one end, leaving a tail, which may be darned in later.

Opening up the plies

c Starting on a buckle or ring

- Prepare a set of highly twisted 4 ply cords.
- Take a cord and fold it in half to find the centre point.
- Take one end of the cord through the ring and then take it through itself just below the centre point, by splitting the cord 2 ply ↑ and 2 ply ↓ to form a loop.
- Tighten this looped cord over the ring. Take the other cords in turn and repeat, making sure that they are all mounted on the ring with the cords coming from the loops in the same direction.
- For single cords, take one end of the cord through the ring and then take it through its eye, tighten and discard safety tie.

Start on a D ring, covered with buttonhole stitch

d Single loop start

This is one of several neat ways of starting a ply split braid using the cords alone.

Note the sequence of the cords, as the loop is made with the central folded cord.

- Take a cord and fold it in half to find the centre point. Take one end of the cord through itself just below the centre point 2 ply ↑ and 2 ply ↓ to form a loop.
- Split the doubled cord below its loop 2 ply ↑ and 2 ply ↓ and add a new cord by taking it through both splits and even up the cord lengths.
- Proceed by adding each new cord, see Diagrams 4 a and b.

Diagram 4a and b Single Loop Start.

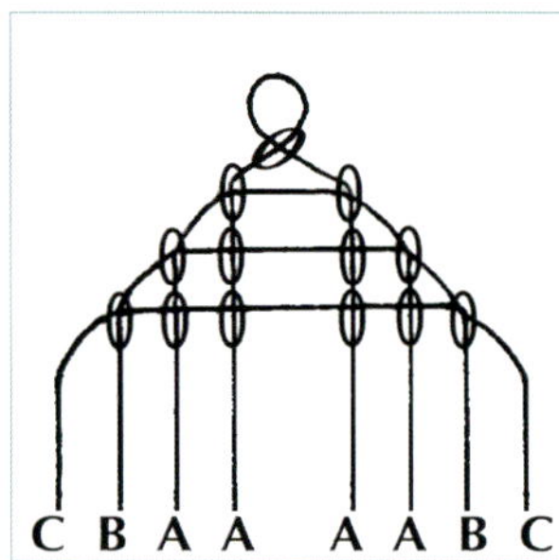

About the designs

The best way to become familiar with a new technique is to make a series of samples using the basic methods. By following the designs in this book in order, you will build up your ply-splitting skills. These samples will give you a basic vocabulary of shapes that can be used on their own or in combination to make interesting textile braids, jewellery and accessories.

The samples have been made using highly twisted 4 ply cords made from four lengths (elements) of double knitting (DK) cotton and I recommend that you use this or something similar, for your initial samples.
By using coloured cords in the suggested sequences the structure of the braid will become apparent.

Doubled cords are used in most of the samples described and may be started either from a central loop, as shown or on a rod or ring. It is assumed that the split is made with a quarter twist, the usual method of splitting 4 ply cords, unless otherwise stated. See Splitting the Plies on page 8.

Two new plies are always split when splitting the previous row's splitter.

Occasionally cords are split taking the next two new plies 2 ply ↑ & 2 ply ↓
This is known as a half twist and is useful when taking a cord back on itself, around a corner, as in Waves and Zigzag. A half twist is also used for twined linking. See Finishing braids on page 33.
If a half twist is used consistently it will make a braid with ridges and furrows.

The Notation

Number 1 refers to the first placed cord on the left and 8 (or high number) the last cord on the right.

The cords travel but the number sequence always stays the same, so counting starts again at the start of each row.

The symbol **>** means that a cord (the splitter) goes through or splits the ply of the numbered cord.

Turn means that the whole piece is turned over, like the page of a book.

In diagrams ⬯ denotes a splittee - a cord, being split by another cord.

For further notes on terminology see the Glossary of Terms on page 45

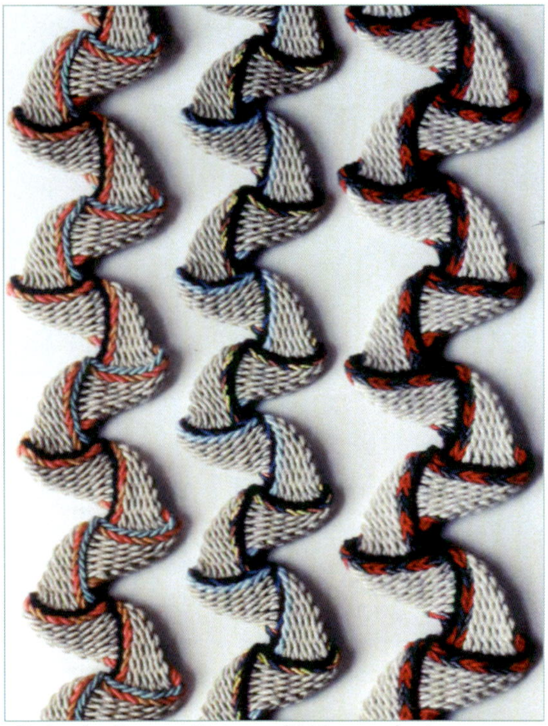
Belts in linen, Oriental Waves design

Belt in cotton, Basket Weave design

Belt in linen, Waves design

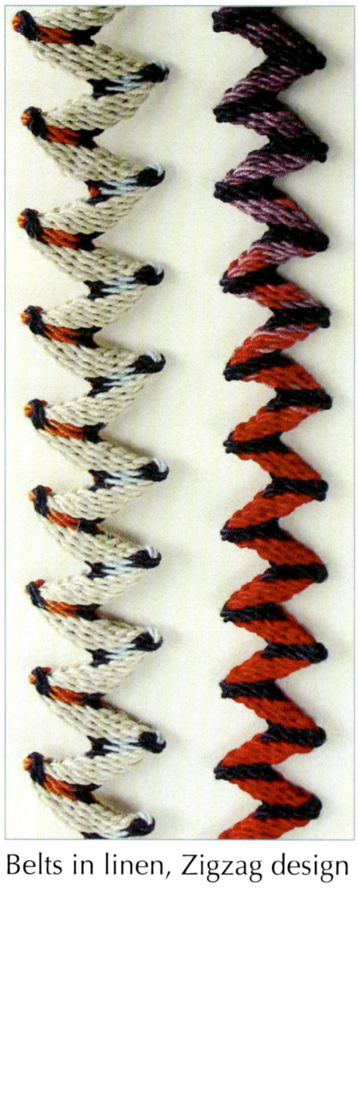
Belts in linen, Zigzag design

Diagonal Stripe
Chevron
Waves
Oriental Waves
Waves Spiral

Neckpiece 'South China Seas' by Dr Ann Brammer, Spiral Waves with beads. photo Jennie Parry

Diagonal Stripe

In this basic ply- split braid a range of colours is used to make a braid with a diagonal stripe and fell.

Prepare 4 ply cords in 3 colours, A,B,C to the required length. Cut and seal ends with PVA glue or tape.

Suggested lengths for sample:

A = 2 x 50 cm cords, doubled to make 4 cords x 25 cm
B = 1 x 50 cm cord, doubled to make 2 cords x 25 cm
C = 1 x 50 cm cord, doubled to make 2 cords x 25 cm

Single loop start

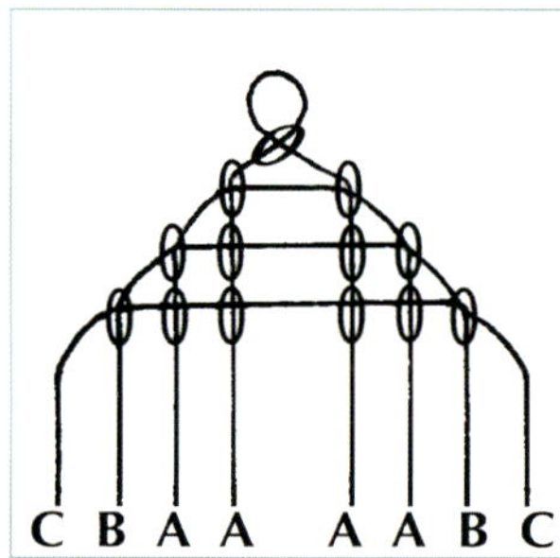

Diagram 5.

To Set up the cords with a single loop start see Diagram 5:
To Spit the plies see Diagram 1 on page 8 and repeated below.

- Take an **A** cord and fold it in half to find the centre point.
- Take one end of the cord through itself just below the centre point 2 ply ↑ and 2 ply ↓ to form a loop.
- Split the doubled cord below its loop 2 ply ↑ and 2 ply ↓ and add the other **A** cord by taking it through both splits and even up the cord lengths.
- Proceed by adding the **B** cord, followed by the **C** cord to get:

Start order (1)**CBAAAABC**(8)

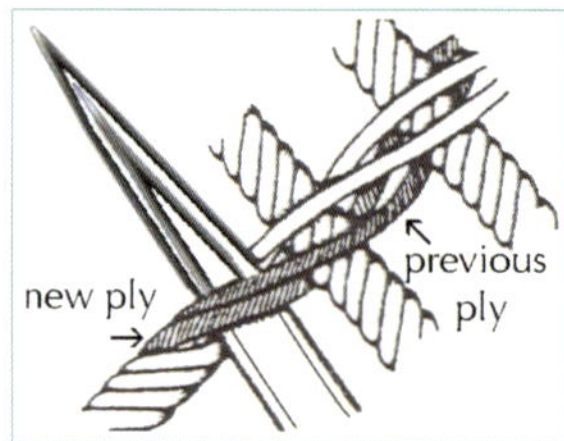

2 ply ↑ 2 ply ↓ leaving a quarter twist

For row 1, start by taking the gripfid through > 2 new plies of cord 8 and take the next new ply plus the adjacent previous ply, leaving a quarter twist, on cords 7,6,5,5,3,2 from right to left with 2 ply ↑ and 2 ply ↓.
Take cord 1, the splitter (without splitting it) directly > the 7 other cords, the splittees.

Row 1

For rows 2 - 8 repeat by taking the new number 1 cord > the others from left to right. Pull the splitter evenly tight against the splittees at the end of each row. The colour sequence repeats over 8 rows:

Row 1	**1C > 2B+3A+4A+5A+6A+7B+8C**
Row 2	**1B > 2A+3A+4A+5A+6B+7C+8C**
Row 3	**1A > 2A+3A+4A+5B+6C+7C+8B**
Row 4	**1A > 2A+3A+4B+5C+6C+7B+8A**
Row 5	**1A > 2A+3B+4C+5C+6B+7A+8A**
Row 6	**1A > 2B+3C+4C+5B+6A+7A+8A**
Row 7	**1B > 2C+3C+4B+5A+6A+7A+8A**
Row 8	**1C > 2C+3B+4A+5A+6A+7A+8B**

Repeat from Row 1

Row 2

Tip: Roll the ply against the twist to open up the plies before inserting the gripfid.

Note: This braid curves slightly in the same direction as the twist of the cords. It can be useful when designing for a neckpiece or belt or when a gentle curve is required.

Chevron

This is a miniature version of one of the typical designs used in making camel girths. The girths are several chevrons in width. See picture below. For Double Chevrons design, see Ply-Split Braiding, Further Techniques page 46.

Prepare 4 ply cords in 3 colours, A,B,C to the required length and cut and seal the ends with PVA glue or tape.

A = 2 x 50 cm cords, doubled to make 4 cords x 25 cm
B = 1 x 50 cm cord, doubled to make 2 cords x 25 cm
C = 1 x 50 cm cord, doubled to make 2 cords x 25 cm

Set up the cords with a single loop start as for Diagonal Stripe

Start order CBAAAABC

Rows 1 – 5 are used to get each cord into play and to create the V shaped fell, after which only rows 6 and 7 are repeated. Pull the splitter evenly tight against the splittees at the end of each row.

Note: From row 2 the previous row's splitter is always the first cord to be split at the start of each new row.

Row 1	**4 > 5**	**turn braid over**
Row 2	**3 > 4**	**turn braid over**
Row 3	**3 > 4+5**	**turn braid over**
Row 4	**2 > 3+4**	**turn braid over**
Row 5	**2 > 3+4+5**	**turn braid over**
Row 6	**1 > 2+3+4**	**turn braid over**
Row 7	**1 > 2+3+4+5**	**turn braid over**

Repeat rows 6 and 7 Only

Cotton camel girths for sale at Pushkar Camel Fair 2004. Note the varying colour of the cords.

Diagonal Stripe

Chevron

Note: You will be splitting three cords in one row and four in the next.
Try to: Work with an odd number of cords to make an even braid.
Vary the colour and number of the cords to make wider braids.

Waves

Prepare 4 ply cords in 3 colours, A,B,C to the required length.
Cut and seal ends with PVA glue or tape.

A = 2 x 50 cm cords, doubled to make 4 cords x 25 cm
B = 1 x 50 cm cord, doubled to make 2 cords x 25 cm
C = 1 x 50 cm cord, doubled to make 2 cords x 25 cm

Set the cords up as shown in Diagram 6.

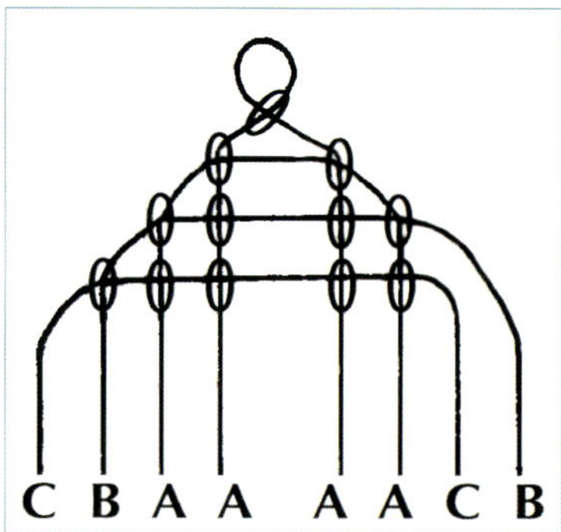

Diagram 6. Set up for Waves and Oriental waves from a single loop start.

Note: The different start order from the previous braid

Start order	**CBAAAACB.**
Row 1	**1C > 2+3+4+5+6+7+8B**
Row 2	**1B > 2+3+4+5+6+7B**
Row 3	**1A > 2+3+4+5+6B**
Row 4	**1A > 2+3+4+5B**
Row 5	**1A > 2+3+4B**
Row 6	**1A > 2+3B**
Row 7	**1C > 2B**

At the end of these rows, pull each splitter very tight to make an exaggerated curve, then **turn** the whole braid over and repeat the sequence.

On the first row after turning, i.e. rows 8, 15, 22 etc. a **half twist** may be left on cord 8, 15, 22 etc. to make a neat base to the wave shape

Note:
In this design colour B shows on the surface edge throughout
and C appears as a dot of colour in the dip below the crest of the wave.

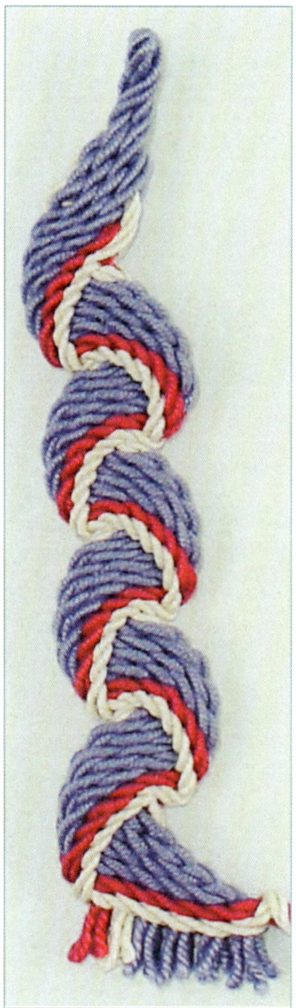

Waves

Oriental waves

This is a variation on the waves design

Prepare 4 ply cords in 3 colours, A,B,C to the required length.
Cut and seal the ends with PVA glue or tape.

A = 2 x 50 cm cords, doubled to make 4 cords x 25 cm
B = 1 x 50 cm cord, doubled to make 2 cords x 25 cm
C = 1 x 50 cm cord, doubled to make 2 cords x 25 cm

Set the cords up as for Waves design. Diagram 6.

Start order CBAAAACB

Tip: In this design, don't pull the splitters tight until the end of the whole section. This will make splitting the plies easier.
Note: The take up of each cord varies within the waves design. To allow for this, the cords may be doubled off-centre at set up.

Section 1

Row 1	**1C > 2+3+4+5+6+7+8B**
Row 2	**1B > 2+3+4+5+6+7B**
Row 3	**1A > 2+3+4+5+6B**
Row 4	**1A > 2+3+4+5B**
Row 5	**1A > 2+3+4B**
Row 6	**1A > 2+3B**
Row 7	**1C > 2B**

At the end of these rows, pull each splitter very tight to make an exaggerated curve, then **turn** the whole braid over.

Work section 1 again, but **don't turn.**

Go to section 2:

Section 2

Row 1	**1B > 2+3+4+5+6+7+8C**
Row 2	**1C > 2+3+4+5+6+7C**
Row 3	**1A > 2+3+4+5+6C**
Row 4	**1A > 2+3+4+5C**
Row 5	**1A > 2+3+4C**
Row 6	**1A > 2+3C**
Row 7	**1B > 2C**

At the end of these rows, pull each splitter very tight to make an exaggerated curve, then **turn** the whole braid over. Work section 2 again, but **don't turn.** Go to section 1.

In brief: **Section 1, turn, section 1 don't turn.**
Section 2, turn, section 2 don't turn.
Repeat.

Note : Colour C shows on the surface edge for two sections followed by colour A showing on the surface edge for two sections.

Spiral Waves

This is another variation on the waves design
Set up as Waves, then

Section 1, pull each splitter very tight and do not turn
Section 2, pull each splitter very tight and do not turn.
Repeat to make a spiral.

Note: Colour C shows on the surface edge for 1 section followed by colour B on the surface edge for one section.

Oriental Waves

From a diagonal stripe into Oriental Spiral in linen

Oriental Spiral in linen

To try: Many further designs can be made by combining Diagonal Stripe and Waves designs. Remember that the colour order you start with is crucial to the resulting design.

Neckpiece in linen, using Zigzag and Waves together

Neckpiece in cotton with space dyed cords, Diagonal Stripe into Zigzag and Waves.

Neckpiece in linen, Diagonal Stripe into Zigzags

Zigzag
Zigzag Flower Shape
Zigzag Spiral
Cogs

Zigzag

Prepare 4 ply cords in three colours

A = 2 x 1 metre, doubled to make 4 cords x 50 cm
B = 1 x 50 cm cord with eye (see Glossary of Terms, page 45)
C = 1 x 50 cm cord with eye

Set up : See Diagram 7

Start order CAAAAB

Note. The last row of set up is the 1st row of section 1

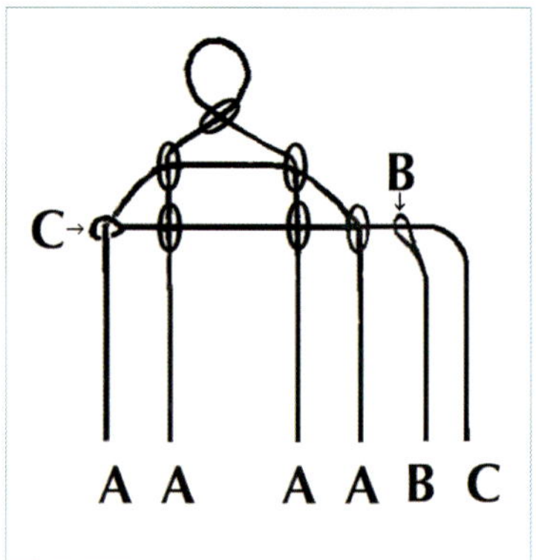

Diagram 7. Set up for Zigzag from a single loop start

Last row of set up,is row 1

* Section 1

Row 1: 1 > 2+3+4+5+6

1 > 2+3+4+5

1 > 2+3+4

1 > 2+3

1 > 2

At the end of this section, pull each splitter tight and **turn** the braid over.

Section 2

5 > 6, leave a half twist on 6 to form point. Pull splitter tight

4 > 5+6, pull splitter tight

3> 4+5+6, pull splitter tight

2 > 3+4+5+6, pull splitter tight

1 > 2+3+4+5+6, pull splitter tight

Don't turn at the end of this section.

Repeat from * Section 1

In brief: Section 1, section 2, section 1 section 2

Note:

The whole colour repeat is over 4 sections.
In the first of sections 1 and 2 colour B will double back on itself to form the centre of one 'Zig'.

In the second repeat colour C will double back on itself to form the centre of the opposite 'Zag', sections 3 and 4.

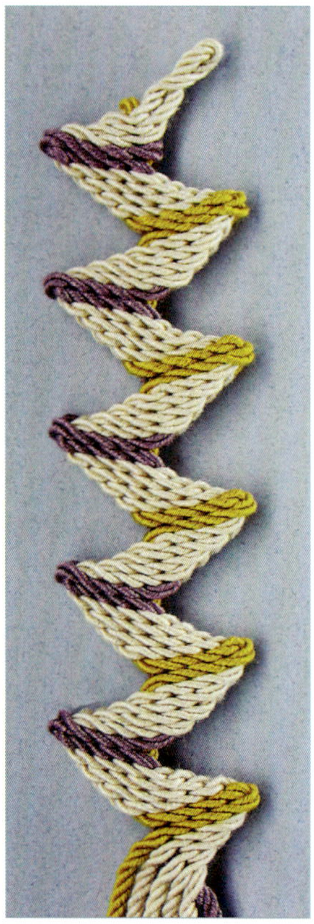

Zigzag

Note: The last splitter (row 5) of section 2 will form the centre of the next Zigzag.
To try: Before starting section 2, put cord 6 through a bead, for added decoration.

Zigzag flower shape

To make a flower shape, the points on one side of the Zigzag braid may be joined during braiding as follows:

- Make sections 1,2,3,4 & 5 of Zigzag
- At the end of section 5 take cord 1 > the point of sections 1 & 2 , made by the doubled back central cord and pull tight before starting row one of section 6.
- At the end of the odd sections 9,13,17,21 take cord 1 > the central cord (point) of the previous sections 5/6,9/10,13/1 & 17/18 before starting row one of the following even section.

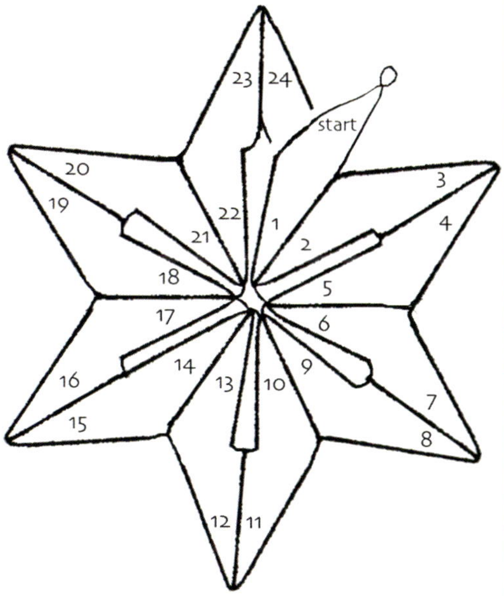

Diagram 8

You may make and join as many sections as you wish to make many petalled flowers. The cord ends may be brought through the centre and cut, be braided together to form a stem or be darned in.

Flower shapes may also be made with Zigzag inner sections and Oriental Waves outer sections.
Explore the possibilities of going from a Diagonal Stripe braid into flower shapes.

Zigzag Flower Shape in linen

Zig-Zag Spiral.

This is A variation on the zigzag design.

Set up as Zigzag or Cogs, see diagram 7 or 9 and work the sections 1 and 2 below.

Start order CAAAAB

Section 1
Pull each splitter tight
Turn the braid over.

Section 2
Pull each splitter tight as you work.
Turn the braid over.

Repeat

Zigzag spiral in linen

Cogs

This design is a combination of Waves and Zigzag designs.

Prepare 4 ply cords in three colours.

A = 3 x 1.5 metre cords, doubled to make 6 cords x 75 cm
B = 1 x 75 cm cord with eye (see Glossary of terms, page 45)
C = 1 x 75 cm cord with eye

Set up: see Diagram 9

Start order C AAAAAAB

Note. The last row of set up is the 1st row of section 1

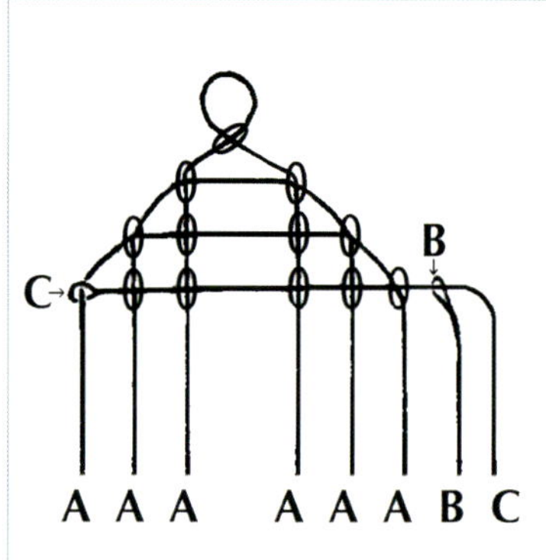

Diagram 9. Set up for cogs from a single loop start

Last row of set up, is row 1

Section 1

1 > 2+3+4+5+6+7+8

1 > 2 +3+4+5+6+7

1 > 2+3+4+5+6

1 > 2+3+4+5

1 >2+3+4

1 >2+3

1>2 pull tight and turn braid over

Repeat section 1

Section 2

7 > 8, pull splitter tight

6 > 7+8, pull splitter tight

5 > 6+7+8, pull splitter tight

4 > 5+6+7+8, pull splitter tight

3 > 4+5+6+7+8, pull splitter tight

2 > 3+4+5+6+7+8, pull splitter tight

1 > 2+3+4+5+6+7+8, pull splitter tight

Don't turn braid over

Go to section 1 and repeat the whole sequence

In brief: section 1, section 1, section 2.

Cogs

Note: The whole colour repeat is over 6 sections. In the first repeat of sections 1,1,2 colour B will double back on itself to form the centre of the first cog. In the second repeat of sections 1,1,2 colour C will double back on itself to form the centre of the next cog.This design has one short and one long edge, making a natural curve. It is an ideal braid for a neckpiece

Thumbprints
Double Thumbprints
Basket Weave Effects

Thumbprints

Prepare 4 ply cords in 3 colours A,B,C, to the required length. Cut the ends and seal with PVA glue. Cords A and B will form the thumbprints and the C cords show as a triangle of colour on the outside edge.

A = 2 cords x 2m doubled to make 4 x 1m cords
B = 2 cords x 2m doubled to make 4 x 1m cords
C = 2 cords x 1.5 m doubled to make 4 x 75 cm cords.

The **C** cords are core cords, consistent splitters, on which the take up is less.

Start order AAAACCCCBBBB

Starting on a rod or ring, set the cords up in doubles, see start order, then arrange the cords into 3 working groups A, B & C as follows;

11 (already through) 10 , 9 ,8 ,7 ,6 ,5 , each > 12, one at a time
11 , 10 , 9 ,8 , 7 , 6 , each > 12, one at a time
11 , 10 , 9 , 8 , 7 , each > 12, one at a time
11 , 10 , 9 , 8 , each > 12, one at a time pull tight

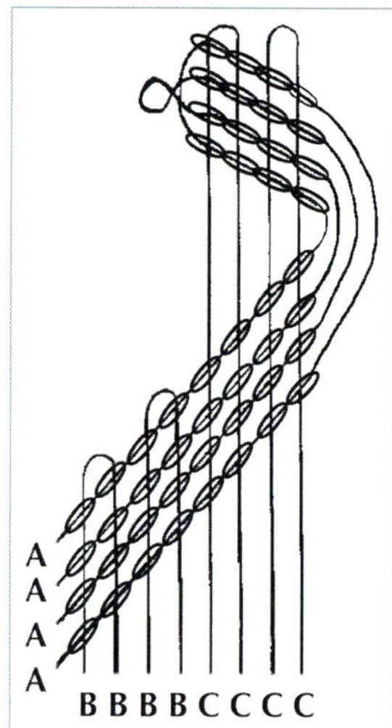

Diagram 10. Thumbprints from a loop start

Thumbprints start on rod

To work from a loop start, set up the cords as shown in Diagram 10, leaving a quarter twist on each intersection, **turn the cords over** and **start at section B** then go through the full repeat.

*** Start of full repeat**

A
1 > 2+3+4+5+6+7+ 8
1 > 2+3+4+5+6+7
1 > 2+3+4+5+6
1 > 2+3+4+5, pull tight & turn

B
1 (C) > 2+3+4+5+6+7+8
1 (C) > 2+3+4+5+6+7
1 (C) > 2+3+4+5+6
1 (C) > 2+3+4+5, pull tight & turn

C
8 (C) > 9+10+11+12, leave half twist on cords 9 & 12
7 (C) > 8+9+10+11
6 (C) > 7+8+9+10
5 (C) > 6+7+8+9, pull very tight to cover core

D
1 > 2+3+4+5+6+7+8
1 > 2+3+4+5+6+7
1 > 2+3+4+5+6
1 > 2+3+4+5, pull tight & turn

E
1 (C) > 2+3+4+5+6+7+8
1 (C) > 2+3+4+5+6+7
1 (C) > 2+3+4+5+6
1 (C) > 2+3+4+5, pull tight & turn

F
8 (C) > 9+10+11+12, leave half twist on cords 9 & 12
7 (C) > 8+9+10+11
6 (C) > 7+8+9+10
5 (C) > 6+7+8+9, pull very tight to cover core

Repeat from *

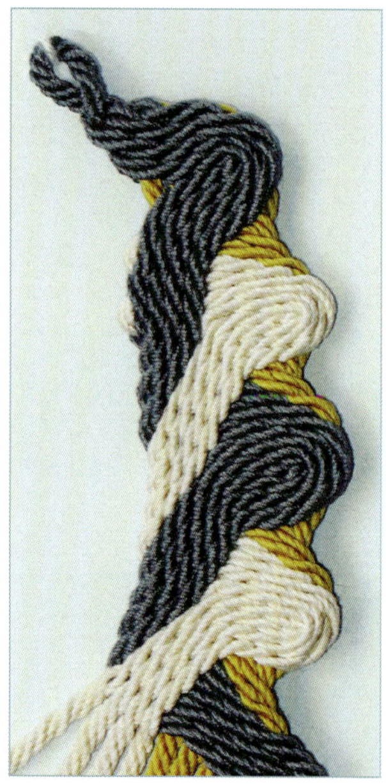

Thumbprints from a loop start showing repeat

The Thumprints design has one short and one long edge, making a natural curve. It is an ideal braid for a neckpiece. The full colour repeat is over 12 sections. This becomes apparent when working with more colours. The inside cord of Thumbprint 1 becomes the outside cord of Thumbprint 3. See Gallery page 41.

Double Thumbprints

Prepare 4 ply cords in three colours.
14 x 4 ply cords in 3 colours (7 doubles)

A = 2 x 1.5 metre cords doubled to make 4 x 75 cm cords
B = 2 x 1.5 metre cords doubled to make 4 x 75 cm cords.
C = 3 x 1 metre cords doubled to make 6 x 50 cm cords,

Note: C = Core cords.
These are consistent splitters, on which the take up is less.

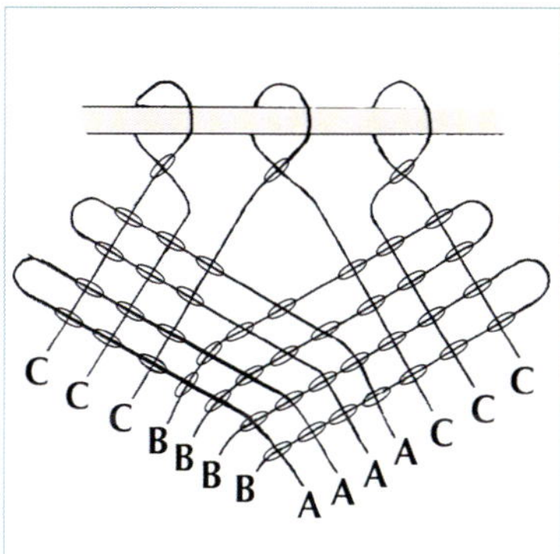

Diagram 11.
set up for DoubleThumbprints

To make a neat start and to get to the required start order, loop the doubled core cords (C) onto a rod and put the 'A' cords directly onto 3 core cords on left and the 'B 'cords directly onto 3 core cords on right See Diagram 11, as follows:

6C, 5C , 4C each > 7B

7C, 6C , 5C each > 8B leaving half twist at loop of last row's 7B with 8B

8C,7C ,6 C each > 9B

9C,8C , 7C each > 10B leaving half twist at loop of last row's 9B with 10B

Pull tight and turn

10C , 9C , 8C each > 11A

11C , 10C , 9C each > 12A leaving half twist at loop of last row's 11A with 12A

12C , 11C ,10C each > 13A

13C , 12C , 11C each > 14A leaving half twist at loop of last row's 13A with 14A

Pull tight and turn to make the start order:

(1)C C C A A A A B B B B C C C(14)

Double Thumbprints 1

See pages, 26 and 27 for design instructions →

Version of Double Thumbprints design 2, coiled for bangle

Double Thumbprints

After set up, see previous page 25, work the following 10 sections.

***Section 1**

7A > 8B + 9B +10B +11B
6A > 7B + 8B +9B + 10B
5A > 6B + 7B +8B + 9B
4A > 5B + 6B +7B + 8B
Pull all A cords tight through B cords

Section 2

3C > 4B +5B +6B +7B
2C > 3B +4B +5B +6B
1C > 2B +3B +4B +5B
Pull all B cords tight over all C cords and **turn**

Section 3

10C > 11B +12B +13B + 14B leave half twist on 14B
9C > 10B +11B +12B +13B
8C > 9B +10B +11B +12B
Pull very tight to cover C core cords to form the Thumbprint 1

Double Thumbprints 1

Section 4

3C > 4A +5A +6A +7A
2C > 3A +4A +5A +6A
1C > 2A +3A +4A +5A
Pull all A cords tight over all C cords and **turn**

Section 5

10C > 11A +12A +13A + 14A leave half twist on 14A
9C > 10A +11A +12A +13A
8C > 9A +10A +11A +12A
Pull very tight to cover C core cords to form Thumbprint 2

Section 6

7B > 8A + 9A +10A +11A
6B > 7A + 8A +9A + 10A
5B > 6A + 7A +8A + 9A
4B > 5A + 6A +7A + 8A
Pull all B cords tight over all A cords

Section 7

3C > 4A +5A +6A +7A
2C > 3A +4A +5A +6A
1C > 2A +3A +4A +5A
Pull all A cords tight over all C cords and **turn**

Section 8

10C > 11A +12A +13A + 14A leave half twist on 14A
9C > 10A +11A +12A +13A
8C > 9A +10A +11A +12A
Pull very tight to cover C core cords to form Thumbprint 3

Start of belt in Double Thumbprints design 2.

Note: By pulling the core cords very tight, the braid will curve in.
To try: Use different numbers of core cords and working cords to make other thumbprint shapes.

Section 9

3C > 4B +5B +6B +7B
2C > 3B +4B +5B +6B
1C > 2B +3B +4B +5B
Pull all B cords tight over all C cords and Turn

Section 10

10C > 11B +12B +13B + 14B leave half twist on 14B
9C > 10B +11B +12B +13B
8C > 9B +10B +11B +12B
Pull very tight to cover C core cords to form Thumbprint 4

Repeat from * (Section 1)

Double Thumbprints 2

With colour B showing on the surface as linked thumbprints and colour A as broken thumbprints the braid is formed as follows :
Work on sections 1 – 5 above but at the end of section 5 pull very tight to cover C core cords to form Thumbprint and **Turn**
Repeat sections 1 – 5 in this way.

Double Thumbprints 2

Double Thumbprints 3

Forming individual  shapes of colour B on a background of A.

Work on the above sections in the following sequence:
Section 1 , 2 , 3 , 4 , 5 , 6, 4 , 5 , 2 , 3 , 1 , 2 , 3 , 4 , 5 and **turn. Repeat**

Double Thumbprints 3

Basket Weave Effects

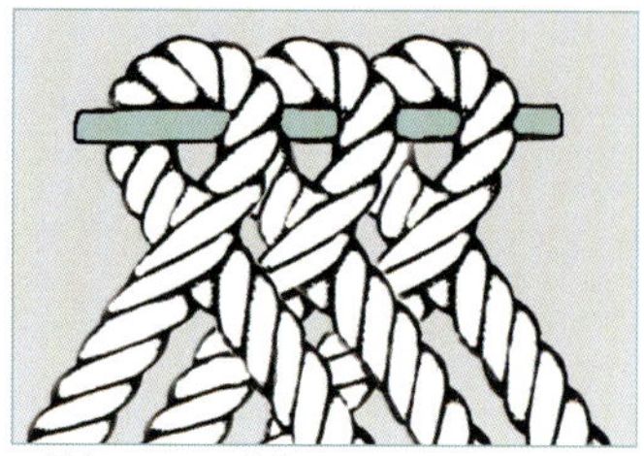

Diagram 12.
Set up from rod start

This section includes some variations using blocks of intersecting cords.
Prepare 4 ply cords in 2 colours to the required length and cut and seal the ends with PVA glue.

A = 4 cords doubled to make 8 cords
B = 4 cords doubled to make 8 cords

Set up the cords on a rod, pin or buckle. see Diagram 12. See start order.
Cord 1 and 16 A may be one cord taken along the rod through the loop made by the other cords.
This sequence gives 4 blocks of cords of ABBA but other colour blocks could be used.
E.g. blocks of AAAA, BBBB, ABAB, or combinations of these.

Start order 1A B B A A B B A A B B A A B B A16

In this design the cords are grouped into 4 sets of 4 cords by the following sequence.

Set up of blocks

1 > 2+3+4+5+6+7+8 . 1 > 2+3+4+5+6+7. 1 > 2+3+4+5+6. 1 > 2+3+4+5

15,14,13,12,11,10,9 each > 16,one at a time .

15, 14, 13, 12 , 11,10 each > 16, one at a time

15,14,13,12,11, each >16, one at a time.

15,14,13,12, each > 16,one at a time
Turn over

Basket Weave 1

In this design small 4 cord rectangular interlocking blocks are made.

Basket Weave 1

***Section 1**
8 > 9+10+11+12. 7 > 8+9+10+11. 6 > 7+8+9+10.
5 > 6+7+8+ 9
Do not turn

Section 2
1 > 2+3+4. 1 > 2+3. 1 > 2. Do not turn

Section 3
15, 14,13 each > 16, one at a time, leaving a half twist on 16.
15,14 each > 16, one at a time
15 >16. Turn

Section 4
4 > 5+6+7+8. 3 > 4+5+6+7. 2 > 3+4+5+6. 1 > 2+3+4+5.
Do not turn

Section 5
12>13+14+15+16, leaving a half twist on 16
11>12+13+14+15
10>11+12+13+14
9>10+11+12+13. Turn

REPEAT from *

Basket Weave 2

In this design longer interlocking rectangles are produced.

Start order and set up are the same as Basket Weave 1 or you may wish to continue from the end of Basket Weave 1. If you do this make sure you turn the braid over at the end of Basket Weave 1, section 5.

Basket Weave 2

*** Section 1**

8 > 9+10+11+12. 7 > 8+9+10+11. 6 > 7+8+9+10. 5 > 6+7+8+ 9 Do not turn

Section 2

1 > 2+3+4. 1 > 2+3. 1 > 2. Do not turn

Section 3

15,14,13 each > 16, one at a time , leaving a half twist on 16.

15,14 each > 16, one at a time

15 >16 Do not turn.

By not turning the braid over at this point longer interlocking rectangles are achieved.

Section 4

4 > 5+6+7+8. 3 > 4+5+6+7. 2 > 3+4+5+6. 1 > 2+3+4+5. Do not turn

Section 5

12>13+14+15+16, leaving a half twist on 16

11>12+13+14+15. 10>11+12+13+14

9>10+11+12+13. Turn

REPEAT from *

Basket Weave Designs

Left: 4 ply cords in 3/12 natural linen.

Centre: 4 ply cords in 8/5 rug warp linen.

Right: 4 ply cords in 3/8 linen with 8 strands per element.

To Try: Vary the number, size or colour of cords in the sets. Work with more sets of cords to make wider braids.

Basket Weave 3

This design is a combination of Basket Weave 1 & 2 & has small 4 cord blocks on one edge and longer interlocking rectangles on the other edge.

Start order and set up as Basket Weave 1.
Work the sections in the following order.

Basket Weave 3

*** Section 1**

8 > 9+10+11+12. 7 > 8+9+10+11. 6 > 7+8+9+10. 5 > 6+7+8+ 9 Do not turn

Section 2

1 > 2+3+4. 1 > 2+3. 1 > 2. Do not turn

Section 3

15, 14,13 each > 16, one at a time , leaving a half twist on 16.
15,14 each > 16, one at a time
15 >16 Do not turn

Section 5

12>13+14+15+16 leaving a half twist on 16
11>12+13+14+15. 10>11+12+13+14. 9>10+11+12+13. Turn

Section 5

12>13+14+15+16 leaving a half twist on 16
11>12+13+14+15. 10>11+12+13+14.
9>10+11+12+13 Do not turn

Section 2

1 > 2+3+4. 1 > 2+3. 1 > 2 Turn

Section 2

1 > 2+3+4. 1 > 2+3. 1 > 2 Do not turn

Section 1

8 > 9+10+11+12. 7 > 8+9+10+11. 6 > 7+8+9+10 .
5 > 6+7+8+ 9 Turn

Section 4

4 > 5+6+7+8. 3 > 4+5+6+7. 2 > 3+4+5+6. 1 > 2+3+4+5.
Do not turn

Section 5

12>13+14+15+16 leaving a half twist on 16. 11>12+13+14+15
10>11+12+13+14. 9>10+11+12+13. Turn

Repeat from *

Estimating Cord lengths for a finished braid

Finishing Braids

Making Cords for use in Ply-Splitting

Designing Cords

Cord length calculations

Estimating Cord lengths for a finished braid

After your initial sampling you will be keen to make a finished braid.
Think about:

- The type of yarn and thickness of cords to use and select appropriate ones for your project
- Varying the number of cords you use to make wider braids
- Experimenting with different colour combinations
- Using single and double cords together
- Using some striped cords with the braid
- Working with elements of two or more designs in one braid
- Varying the size of groups of cords within a design, e.g. Thumbprints and Basket Weave.

Having sampled, you will realise that the amount of take up on the cords varies according to the yarn and cords used and the design. There is also sometimes a variation of take up on individual cords within a design.

Calculating the length of cords to use for a belt, neckpiece, bracelet

1 Make a sample of the design in the yarn and cords selected for the final piece, noting the starting length of the cords and the finished length of the sample.

2 Work out the required finished length of your final piece and multiply up from your sample lengths, allowing for take up and ties, fringes or darning in ends. Always allow some extra length, as it is difficult and not advisable to join in new cords, when braiding a repeating pattern.
Remember: the time taken in braiding is always going to be more valuable than the cost of your cords.

Example for a belt in Chevron design

Make a sample in Chevron design.

4 cords @ 50 cm doubled = 8 cords x 25 cm

Finished sample = 15 cm

Take up = 10 cm on each cord

The finished length of the belt is 90 cm =15 cm x 6.
Allow at least 25 cm x 6 = 150 cm for each cord, or 4 x 3m doubled = 8 cords x 150 cm.
Add approx 25 cm per cord extra . You will need 4 cord lengths of 3.5 metres.

For the Waves design the take-up on each cord within the design varies and this must be taken into account. When doubling the cords at the start of a braid, they can be divided off centre. This can be helpful when calculating the length of cords for braiding a long piece in Waves and similar designs.

Finishing Braids

Securing cords through a splittee and darning in

In the picture, the yellow cord becomes a splittee and prevents the other cords, the splitters, from fraying when cut. To secure the splittee, darn it back through the previous row, pull tight and cut .

Each cord is taken > a splittee then darned back into a previous row

Fringes or tufted ends

Splitter cords may be cut and combed to form tufts or fringes

Tufted ends & twined linking

Twined Linking

Take 2 cords alternately through each other several times, then knot or whip the cords. See Diagram 13.

Diagram 13

Use cords to fasten through starting ring or loop

Darn in one or more cords to secure them, then take the remaining cords through the starting ring or loop to fasten as ties, or leave as decorative cords.

Use a bead to fasten through the starting loop or ring

Secure the cords by taking each through a splittee. Cut all but the splittee cord. Take this cord through a bead and do twined linking into itself, before darning it back into the braid to secure.

Whipping

Form a U shaped loop along the cord or cords to be covered using a fine thread.
With this thread, wrap tightly over the loop from the open end towards the loop end and take the end of the thread (B) through the loop. Diagram 14a. Pull the (A) end tightly to draw the loop behind the whipping and pull A and B ends tightly against each other to hide the 2 loops beneath the whipping. Cut the ends. Diagram 14b.

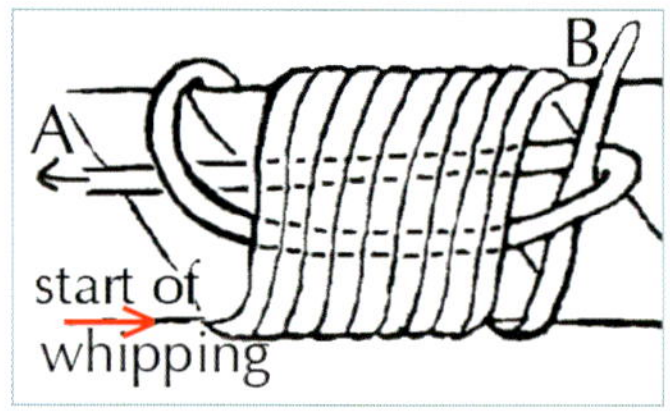

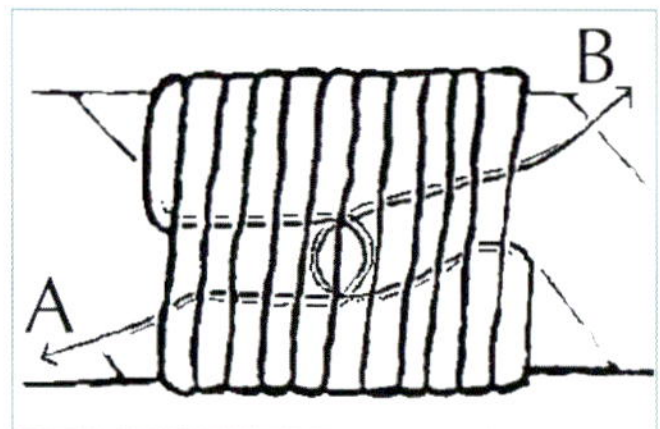

Diagram 14a and b. Whipping

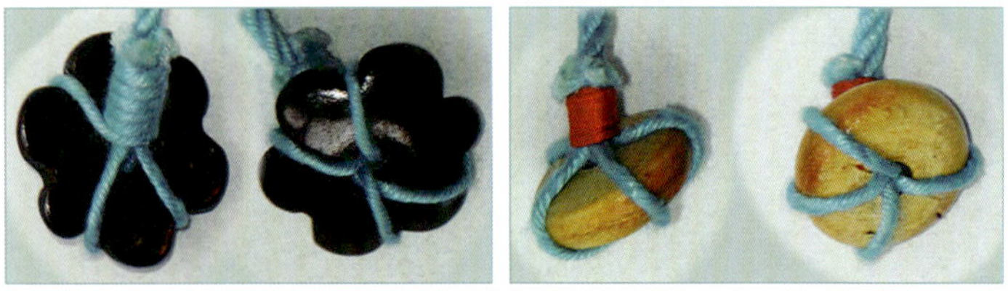

4 ply cord taken through bead, split and whipped

The wrapped or constrictor knot Diagram 15.

Using 1 of the cords, wrap it 3 or 4 times over your thumb,or gripfid lying along side the cords to be covered.
Slip out your thumb or gripfid and take the end of the cord back through the loops made and tighten up

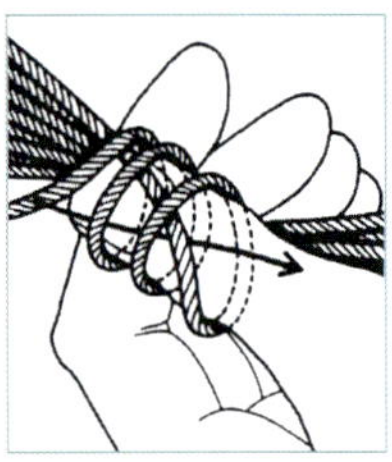

Diagram 15. The wrapped or constrictor knot

Crown knot Diagram 16

Using 4 or more cords, make one or more crown knots to secure the cords, then darned back up the braid. These knots may be made around a central group of cords.

Diagram16. Crown knot using 4 cords

Making Cords for use in Ply-Splitting

The use of highly twisted, usually 4 ply cords, is fundamental to the design and structure of ply-split braids. The choice of yarn and the cord making process determine the quality of these cords. Ideally the yarns used in cord making should be smooth and non hairy. Fine yarn may be used as multiple ends per element or thicker yarn may be used as a single end per element. Other materials e.g. tape, paper, cloth strips, raffia may be used. By sampling you will soon become adept at yarn selection. See Terms used in making cords, page 44.

There are a number of ways to make four ply cords, two of which are described here:

1. Using a single hook in a Hand Drill

2. Using a cord winder with 4 hooks mounted on a rotating head.

There are two essentials stages in cord making which apply to both methods:

Stage One: **Initial Over Twist (IOT)**

Stage Two: **Controlled Counter Twist (CCT)**

See Terms used in making cords on page 44.

Using a hand drill

You will need:

- 1 hand drill + cup hook
- For the Near End: warping post with hook + G clamp
- For the Out End: 2 cup hooks on a block or warping post + G clamp
- 8 'S' hooks or paper clips
- Scissors

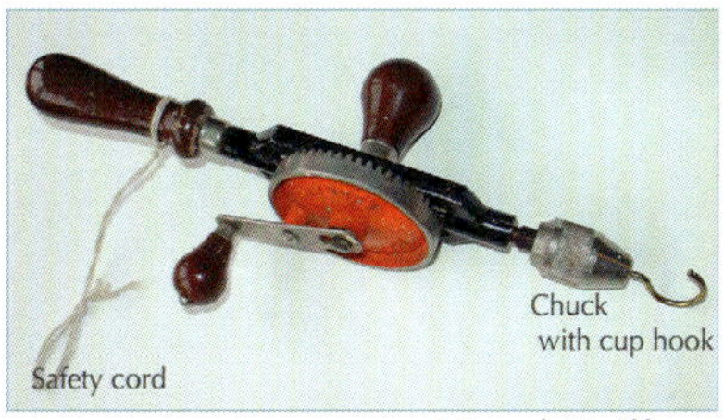

Hand Drill

Set Up

- Secure a large cup hook into the chuck of the hand drill. Tie a safety cord to the handle, made with a loop. Place over a hook mounted on a block or post clamped to the top of a weighted kitchen or tea trolley or table. This is known as the Near End.

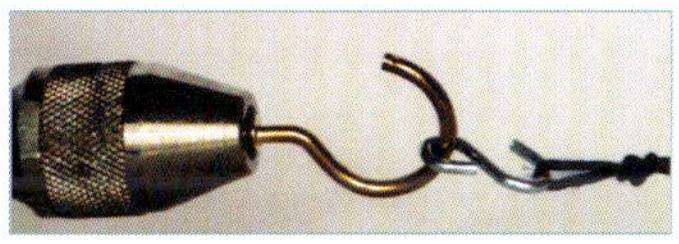
Chuck of hand drill and hook

- Set up an Out End with two cup hooks, 6 cm apart and at the same height, mounted on a block or warping post base, clamped to a second static table. The distance from the hand drill is determined by the length of the required cord + approx. 25% or the length of your room. See notes on cord length calculations on page 39

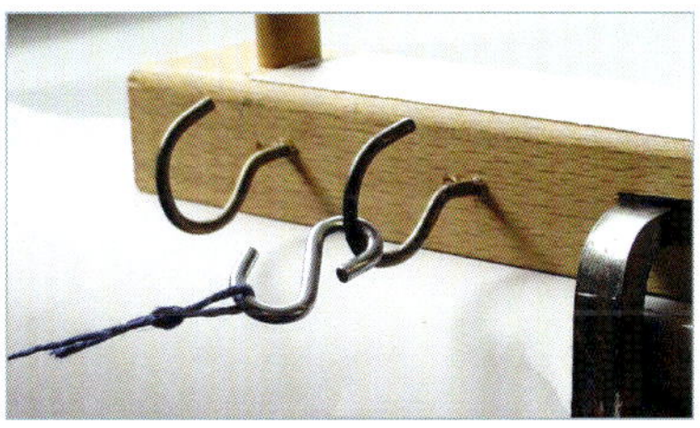
Out End

To make 2, 3, or 4 ply cords:

- Measure 2, 3, or 4 lengths of yarn or multiple ends (for 2, 3, or 4 ply cord) by taking the yarn from the hand drill hook at the Near End to one of the Out End hooks.
- Take one of the single or multiple elements and place onto an 'S' hook using an overhand knot onto the cup hook in the hand drill at the Near End.Tie the other end of the element onto a second 'S' hook and place onto 1 of the 2 cup hooks at the Out End.

Continued on page 36

Initial Over Twist : IOT, using a hand drill

Check the twist of the elements. Is it **S** or **Z** ? see Glossary of Terms on page 45.
Remove the hand drill from the Near End hook.
Holding the hand drill under tension, turn the handle in the appropriate direction (see below) while walking slowly forward towards the Out End.

Right–handed use:

- Hold the hand drill in your left hand and the rotating handle in your right hand.
- Turn the rotating handle away from you (clockwise) for 'S' IOT
- Turn the rotating handle towards you (anticlockwise) for 'Z' IOT

Left–handed use:

- Hold the hand drill in your right hand and the rotating handle in your left hand.
- Turn the rotating handle towards you (clockwise) for 'S' IOT
- Turn the rotating handle away from you (anticlockwise) for 'Z' IOT

To achieve an even tension, lean against the cord slightly while walking. Roll the trolley forward as you walk. Count the number of turns made. See the notes on Cord Length Calculations, page 39.

When the required IOT is achieved (when the element starts to snarl if the tension is relaxed) take it on its 'S' hook from the hand drill and place it on the hook at the Near End, while maintaining the tension of the element.

Walk to the Out End and place the element on its 'S' hook onto the second hook at the Out End, maintaining the tension of the element at all times. Repeat the above for the further 1, 2 or 3 elements (for 2, 3, or 4 ply cord) placing them on top of the first taut element.

Note: The Near End, on the trolley, will have moved nearer the Out End and will be in a new, fixed, position after element 1 has been twisted.The amount of IOT given to each of the other elements can be judged be measuring the length of take up against the first taut element.

Controlled Counter Twist, CCT, using a hand drill

Put all the elements, on their 'S' hooks, back onto the cup hook in the hand drill at the Near End, maintaining the tension and making sure that they are lying parallel and are not snarled. Apply CCT by turning the rotating handle in the opposite direction, while maintaining the tension of the elements.
Slip the cord off the 'S' hooks at each end & tie with overhand knots to avoid unravelling.

Note: When using a Hand Drill, the number of turns required per metre for a specific yarn will be more using the hand drill than using a geared 4 hook cord winder, as the ratio is only 1 : 1.
Note also that when using the hand drill method, the direction of turning the rotating handle for CCT is opposite to that of the IOT.

A range of 4 ply striped cords in 3 colours

Waves design using striped and plain cords

Using a 4 hook hand winder

The following describes the use of a Kipu 4 hook cord winder but the same principles apply to 4 hook winders in general.

When the rotating handle is turned with the brake on (locked) each of the 4 cup hooks turns independently in the same direction. When the brake pin is withdrawn, the whole drum head turns in the opposite direction.

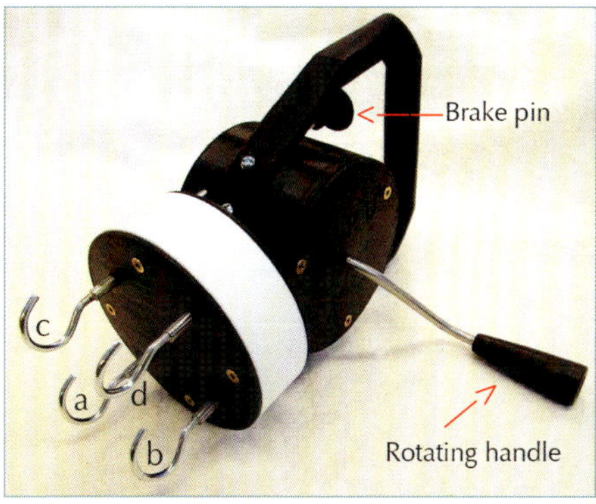

The Kipu Cord Winder

You will need:

- 1 Four hook cord Winder,
- Warping post or hook for Near End
- Out End block with 4 hooks and G clamps
- Scissors
- Short length of thread for tying through eye of cord, approx 7cm (3")

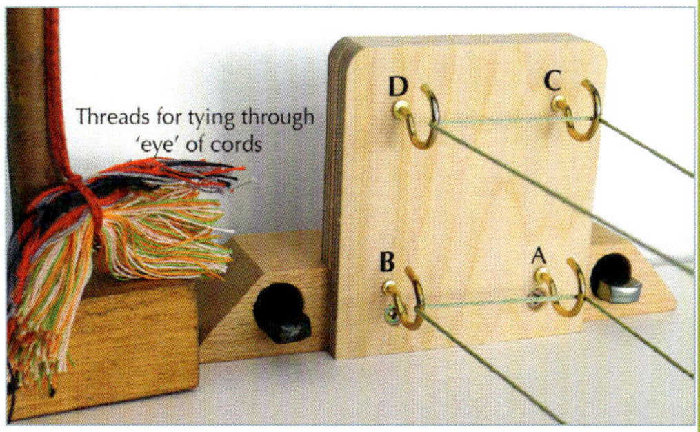

Out end and threads for tying through 'eye' of cord

See Notes on terms used in making cords page 44.

Set up of cord winder:

- Place the 4 hook winder on a table, or preferably a weighted kitchen or tea trolley, attaching the safety cord to a hook or warping post.
- Clamp a 4 hook 'Out End' onto a static solid table at about waist height. The distance from the winder is determined by the length of the required cord + approx 25% or the length of your room. See notes on Cord length calculations on page 39.

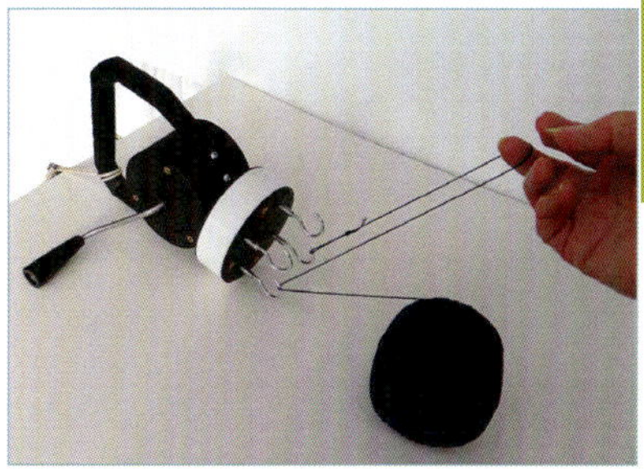
Drawing out 3 elements at once

To make a 4 ply cord:

- Having set up the winder and Out End as above and with the brake pin inserted into the drum,
- Take a length of yarn or multiple ends and tie, using an overhand knot, onto hook 'a' on the winder.
- Draw out the element under tension and loop around hooks 'a' and 'b' on the Out End and return to tie the element onto hook 'b' on the winder. Two parallel elements are in place.
- Repeat this from hook 'c' on the winder, around 'c' and 'd' on the Out End and back to 'd' on the winder. Make sure that each of the 4 elements is parallel and evenly tensioned.
- Cut any loose ends after tying to avoid tangling.
- If using one colour, this process may be simplified by tying a length of yarn onto hook 'a' on the winder, drawing out 3 elements at once to the Out End and looping them around hooks 'a' 'b' 'c' and 'd' before walking back with the 4th element. Cut and tie elements b, c and d making sure that each of the 4 elements is parallel and evenly tensioned.

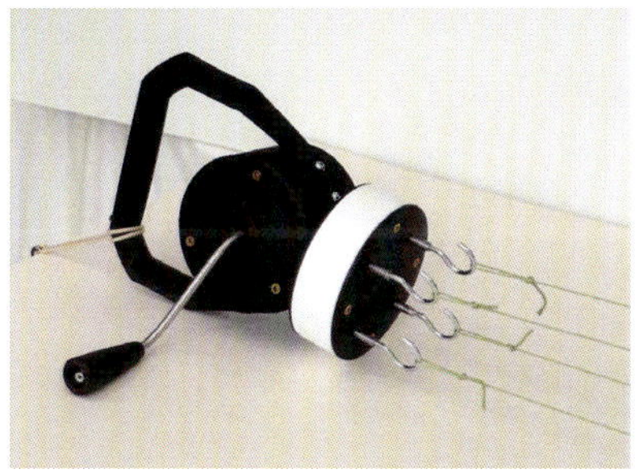
Set up of Kipu winder with one element per hook

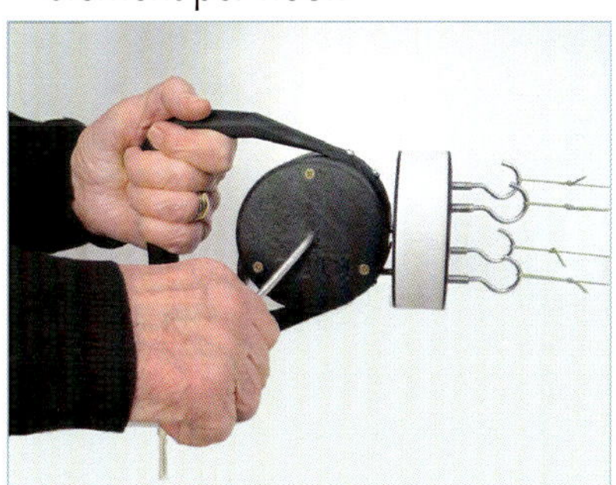
A right-hander putting in IOT

Instructions continued on page 38 →

Tip: It is always easier to set up the elements on the lower hooks first

Initial Over Twist: IOT, using a 4 hook hand winder

Check the twist of the elements. Is it S or Z ? See Glossary of Terms on page 45. Remove the winder from the Near End hook. With the brake pin in the locked position, hold the winder under tension and turn the rotating handle in the appropriate direction (see below) while walking slowly forward towards the Out End.

Right–handed use:

Hold the winder in your left hand and the rotating handle in your right hand.
Turn the rotating handle towards you (anticlockwise) for 'S' IOT
Turn the rotating handle away from you (clockwise) for 'Z' IOT

Left–handed use:

Hold the winder in your right hand and the rotating handle in your left hand.
Turn the rotating handle away from you (anticlockwise) for 'S' IOT.
Turn the rotating handle towards you (clockwise) for 'Z' IOT

Putting in the IOT:

To achieve an even tension, lean against the cord slightly while walking. Roll the trolley forward as you walk. Count the number of turns made. (see Cord length calculations, page 39.)

Return the winder 's safety cord to its hook, when the required IOT is achieved, i.e. when the elements start to snarl if the tension is relaxed.

Go to the Out End, place the loops from a, b and c, d onto the central or single hook and tie a short thread through the eye formed by the loops to prevent unravelling.

Controlled Countertwist : CCT

Return to the winder and holding it as before, while keeping it under tension, release the brake pin and let the handle rotate in the same direction as before, slowly at first, increasing speed gradually to ensure the correct order of the plies. It is helpful to guide the turn of the drum initially.

It is not necessary to count the turns of the CCT, but note that the cord will increase in length slightly as twist is taken out of each element, before decreasing in length again as the counter twist causes the elements to twist against each other into a single 4 ply cord.

Make sure that all excess twist is taken out and that the elements are well embedded by giving the cord extra counter twist. This will result in a cord with a balanced twist opposite to that of the IOT.

Insert the brake pin. Slip the cord off the hooks at the winder and tie with an overhand knot.

The eye end can then be slipped off the Out End.

Note: When using a 4 hook cord winder:

The number of turns required per metre for a specific yarn will be less using a 4 hook winder than a hand drill. This is the case for both initial over twist (IOT)and controlled countertwist (CCT) (i.e.with and without the brake pin inserted) The number of turns of the crank handle required per metre for a specific yarn will also depend on the gear ratio of the winder.

Note:

The Apollo winder has a gear ratio of 4 : 1.The hooks spin at four times the speed of the crank handle

The Kipu winder had a gear ratio of 8 : 1. The hooks spin at eight times the speed of the crank handle

Note on cord construction.

When using a single end of yarn per element the cord construction will be either:

s , s , Z	Initial end(s) S twist,	S twist IOT,	Z twist CCT,	resultant Z twist cord:

or

z , z , S	Initial end(s) Z twist,	Z twist IOT,	S twist CCT,	resultant S twist cord.

This is called a Twist on Twist cord.

Do not attempt to mix the use of single ends of S and Z yarn for the elements of one cord as unravelling, and annoyance will occur!

The following construction is useful and most often used when both S and Z cords are required in one type of yarn. It is only possible using multiple ends per element. It is called a Twist against Twist Cord.

z , s , Z	Initial ends Z twist,	S twist IOT , Z twist CCT,	resultant Z twist cord
s , z , S	Initial ends S twist,	Z twist IOT , S twist CCT,	resultant S twist cord

Designing Cords and Cord Length Calculations

There are two ways to establish consistent cords of the same twist and length.

1. By counting the Turns Per Metre (TPM);
2. By measuring the length of take up, or percentage of initial length.

Counting the TPM:

- On a 4 m setting-up length of Double Knit (DK, Sirdar) 'S' twist cotton.
  Using an Apollo winder, with a gear ratio of 4 - 1
  240 turns of extra 'S' twist is put in (IOT)
- After the CCT the length of the resultant 'Z' cord is 3m 20cm.
- This yarn requires 60 TPM (240 ÷ 4 = 60 TPM)
- The take-up over 4m = 80 cm, for this yarn.
- **Using a Kipu winder,** with a gear ratio of 8 - 1, you will need half the number of turns - 120 turns on 4 metres. (30TPM)

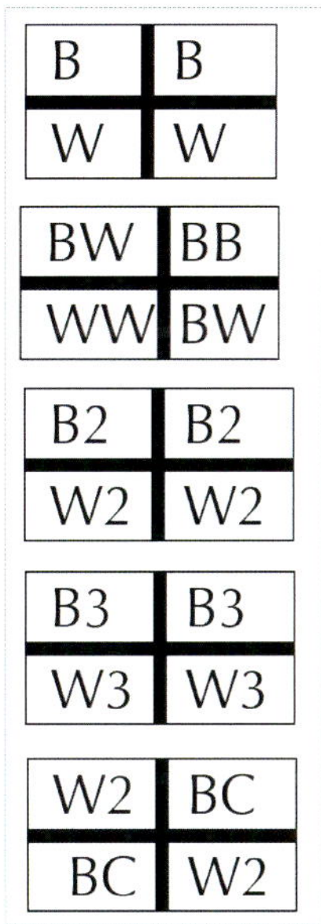

4 ply cord with 2 black and 2 white elements

Blending colours on two of the elements

2 ends per element

3 ends per element

Setting up the pairs of elements on corresponding diagonal hooks on the winder and out end.

Diagram 16.
Notation for the make-up of cords

It is important to sample each yarn to establish the turns needed and the take-up.

Measuring the length of take-up:

- Measure the length of the elements at set up and again after IOT to establish consistent IOT, and again after CCT.

The length of take-up is usually about 20-25% and this can be established for each yarn by sampling.

Colour combinations

The following are some possible colour combinations using 4 ply cords in three colours.
See picture on page 36 and diagram 17 on page 39:

AAAB	**AABB**	**ABBB**	**ABAB**	**AABC**	**ABAC**
BBBC	**BBCC**	**BCCC**	**BCBC**	**BBAC**	**BABC**
CCCA	**CCAA**	**CAAA**	**ACAC**	**CCAB**	**CACB**

2 ply cords: Use 2 diagonal hooks on both the winder and Out End, to keep the winder balanced

3 ply cords: These can be made using 3 of the hooks on the winder and Out End. Use the 2 lower hooks and a single upper hook on both winder and out end. With three hooks in use, the winder may feel unbalanced.

Keeping records is helpful as a reference. A record gives the recipe for repeating specific cords and is also a valuable key to your sampling. It is a useful notation for the make-up of cords, e.g.when using black and white elements they may be notated notated as shown in Diagram 16.

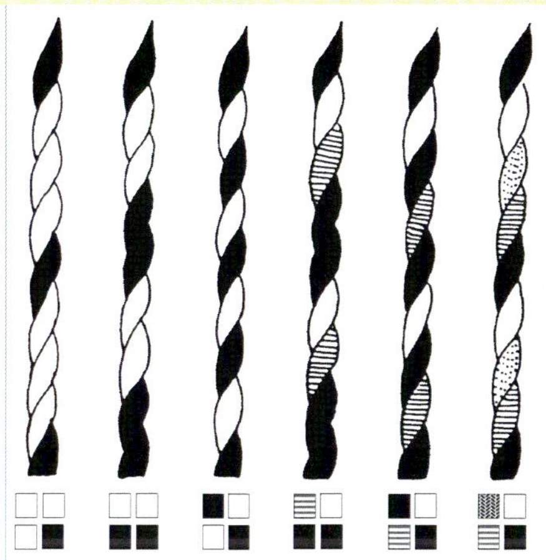

Diagram 17.
4 ply cords, some possibilities

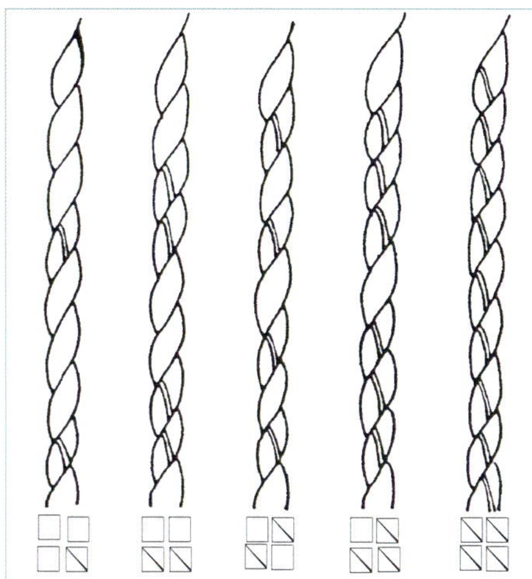

Diagram 18.
4 ply cords with spots or dashes

Other Possibilities:

a

Using a single or multiple ends per element, add an end or ends of a fine yarn, in a contrasting colour or metallic or fancy yarn into one or more of the elements to make spots or dashes. see Diagram 18 and pictures on page 39.

a. Cords with spots of finer yarn.
The pale blue cords are linen.
The yellow/red cords are cotton.

b

To make a series of graded coloured or shaded cords, use multiple ends per element in 2 colours by varying the number of ends of each colour per element, systematically for each cord.

b. A series of shaded cotton cord made from 6 strands per element in 2 colours

c

Work with elements of differing sizes or types of yarn. You may need to adjust the tension of the elements during the IOT stage as the take up of each element may vary

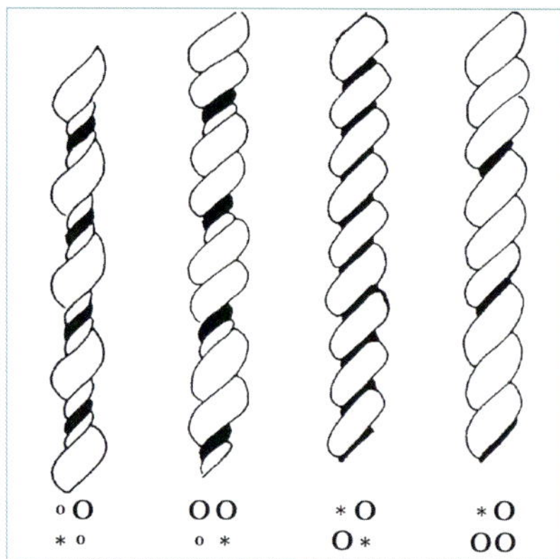

c. 4 ply cords using thick and thin yarns

d

To make complex cords, make 2, 3 or 4 ply cords and then use these as elements to make further cords. Adjust the tension as needed during IOT.

d. Complex cords in cotton and viscose rayon, using thick and thin elements.

Gallery page

Bracelets in linen, Thumbprints design

Neckpiece in linen, Thumbprints design

Neckpiece in linen. Version of cogs design

Bracelets in linen and cotton, versions of double thumbprints.

Neckpiece in linen. Version of Oriental Waves design

Neckpiece in linen. Diagonal stripe and Zigzag design

Neckpiece in linen. Cogs design

Terms used in making cords

Glossary of terms

Suppliers and Resources

Bibliography

Terms used in making cords

Apollo cord winder
The Apollo cord winder has a gear ratio of 4 : 1.
The hooks spin at four times the speed of the crank handle

Controlled Counter Twist (CCT)
The twisting together of the elements in the opposite direction to IOT, under tension to achieve a balanced and Controlled Counter Twist

Element
Individual or multiple ends of yarn which stay coherent throughout the process.

Eye
The loop made by the elements of a cord at the Out End, after CCT.

Hand Drill
Hand Drill with a single hook mounted in the chuck.

Initial end(s) S twist
S twist IOT, **Z** twist CCT, resultant Z twist cord **s, s, Z**

Initial end(s) Z twist
Z twist IOT, **S** twist CCT, resultant S twist cord **z, z, S**

Initial Over Twist (IOT)
Two or more individual or multiple ends of yarn, or other ends, the elements, (e.g. tape, strips of cloth), twisted in the same direction as the original ends, separately in parallel and under tension with appropriate twist for the intended end-use without letting the elements snarl up.

Kipu cord winder
The Kipu winder has a gear ratio of 8 : 1.
The hooks spin at eight times the speed of the crank handle

Multiple ends
Several or many ends of yarn used together as elements in cord making.

Near End
The end at which the elements are looped onto the cord winder or drill.
Also the hook or WP to which the hand drill or cord winder is initially attached.

Out End
The block with hooks, onto which the elements are looped at the furthest point from the cord winder. Usually mounted on a static table.

Single ends
Individual lengths of yarn used as elements in cord making.

Take up
The shortening of the elements that occurs during the twisting process.

TPM
Turns per metre made during the IOT stage.

Twist on Twist Cord
Descriptive of cords made up of single or multiple ends in which the direction of the initial over-twist is the same as that of the fold or spin of the individual ends:

s, s, Z or z, z, S

s , s , Z Initial end(s) S twist, S twist IOT, Z twist CCT, resultant Z twist cord
z , z , S Initial end(s) Z twist, Z twist IOT, S twist CCT, resultant S twist cord

Twist against Twist Cord
Descriptive of cords made up of multiple ends in which the direction of the initial over-twist is counter to that of the fold or spin of the individual ends:

s, z, S or z, s, Z

z , s , Z Initial ends Z twist, S twist IOT, Z twist CCT, resultant Z twist cord.
s , z , S Initial ends S twist, Z twist IOT, S twist CCT, resultant S twist cord.

WP
Warping post, a vertical piece of dowel glued into a block of wood, that is attached to the table or trolley using a G clamp.

Glossary of Terms

In the notation, number 1 refers to the first placed cord on the left and number 8 (or highest number) refers to the last placed cord on the right. The cords travel but the number order always stays the same, so counting starts again at the start of each row. Using 4 ply cords, it is assumed that the split is made with 2 ply above and 2 ply below & a quarter twist is left between rows, unless otherwise stated. In subsequent rows, cords are split with one of the previous ply plus the next ply, to progress down each cord.

> =	This symbol means through in ply splitting. e.g. Cord A **>** (passes through) Cord B or Cord A is the Splitter, Cord B is the Splittee.
↑ =	In ply splitting, means up.
↓ =	In ply splitting, means down.e.g. take Cord A > Cord B with 2 ply↑ and 2 ply ↓
0	In diagrams this symbol denotes Splittee, a cord being split by another cord.
Core Cord	In ply–splitting, a concealed cord which is a consistent splitter.
Doubled cords	Fold a cord over, then split each cord just below its centre, taking one end through the split to make a loop.
Eye	The loop formed at the Out End when making a 4 ply cord. See cord making methods.
Half Twist	Using 4 ply cords, the split is made with 2 ply above and 2 ply below (2 ply ↑ & 2 ply ↓) and they are split with the next 2 new plies, neither having been split in the previous row. This is useful when taking a cord back on itself, around a corner or making a point and when doing twined linking.
Plain(Oblique) Twining	Where each cord alternately splits and is split by each successive cord it crosses
Ply Split Darning	Two sets of cords work in a warp/weft relationship.The warp, or splittees, are split by a weft thread or cord, the splitter or darner.
Quarter Twist	Using 4 ply cords, the split is made with 2 ply above and 2 ply below (2 ply ↑ & 2 ply ↓) They are split with one new ply plus the adjacent previous ply, to progress down each cord.
'S' & 'Z'	The internationally accepted way of describing the direction of twist in a spun or plied thread in relation to its length, which is thought of as the central part of one or other letter **S = ** **Z = /**
Single cords	May be mounted on rod, or buckle by using the Eye formed in cord making.
Single Course (Oblique) Twining	Where a splitter cord passes through two or more successive cords that it crosses in sequence.
Splitter	In ply–splitting, a cord which splits, > (passes through) another cord.
Splittee	In ply–splitting, a cord, which is split by another cord.
Turn	The whole piece is turned over, like the page of a book.
Twined linking	Two cords having been split immediately split each other again

Suppliers and Resources

Yarn Suppliers

Colour Mart
Colourmart Ltd,
www.colourmart.com
Unit 2A, Archers Way,
Battlefield Enterprise Park,
Shrewsbury, SY1 3GA, UK
Supplier of many different yarns
01743 466883

Fairfield Yarns
www.fairfieldyarns.co.uk
Co-operative Buildings,
131 Rochdale Road East,
Heywood, Lancs OL10 1QU
Tel. 01706 623808
Supplier of many different yarns

George Weil, Fibrecrafts
Old Portsmouth Road, Peasmarsh
Guildford, Surrey GU9 2NG
Tel. 01483 565800
www.georgeweil.co.uk
Supplier of yarn and weaving equipment & books

William Hall & Co
www.williamhallyarns.com
177 Stanley Road,
Cheadle Hulme, Cheshire SK8 6RF
Tel. 0161 437 3295
Supplier of Swedish Linens & good quality cotton and rayon yarn

Handweavers Studio & Gallery
www.handweavers.co.uk
140 Seven Sisters Road,
London, N7 7NS
Tel. 020 7272 1891
Supplier of many different yarns & small equipment and books

My Fine weaving Yarns
www.myfineweavingyarn.co.uk
Helen Brotherton
31 Macaulay Road
Lutterworth, Leicestershire
LE17 4XB
Tel. 01455 554647
Supplier of many different yarns

Uppingham Yarns
www.wools.co.uk
30 North Street East,
Uppingham, Rutland, LE15 9QL
Tel. 01572 823747
e.mail uppyarn@wools.co.uk
Supplier of many different yarns

Yeoman Yarns
www.yeoman-yarns.co.uk
Unit 2, Priory Business Park
Wistow Road, Kibworth
Leicester, LE8 0RX
Tel. 0116 2404464
Supplier of yarn, inc Cannele 4 ply Cotton

Resources

The Braid Society
www.braidsociety.com

Braidershand
www.braidershand.com
Washington State USA
Supplier of books, yarn and equipment

Dave Budd
www.davebudd.com
Supplier of gripfids, knives and basket making tools.

Creative Handicraft
www.creativehandicraft.co.uk
e.mail: cordwinders@creativehandicraft.co.uk
Supplier of the Kipu cordwinder and out end

Anna Crutchley
8 Canterbury Street,
Cambridge CB4 3QF
01223 327 685
www.annacrutchley.co.uk
Supplier of hand cord Twister

Louise French
www.louisefrench.com
US Supplier of gripfids, Bradshaw cordwinder head and books on Ply-Split Braiding

Julie Hedges
e.mail juliehedges49@gmail.com
www.juliehedges.co.uk
Books on Ply-Split Braiding, courses in Ply-Split Braiding, commissions. Supplier of Gripfids

Lolox, www.lolox.nl
Dorpsstraat 1
3171 ED Poortugaal
Netherlands
Tel 010-2126959
Supplier of Cord winder head to be attached to a drill, also gripfids.

Bibliography

Berlin, Shirley and McGregor, Ruth, editors
Threads That Move
The Proceedings of the 2nd Conference of Braiding. Manchester 2012. Articles on Ply-Splitting by Julie Hedges, Errol Pires, and Barbara J.Walker.
www.braidsociety.com

Broadbent, Moira
Animal Regalia, 1985
ISBN 0 9510356-0-6

Carey, Jacqui
Braids & Beyond, a broad look at narrow wares.
Published in conjunction with the Braid Society exhibition 2003. ISBN 0 9523225 4 4
Articles on Ply-Splitting by Julie Hedges, Linda Hendrickson, and Barbara Walker.
Available from www.braidsociety.com & www.careycompany.com

Collingwood, Peter
The Techniques of Ply Split Braiding
Bellew Publishing,1998
ISBN 85725 1334

Collingwood, Peter
Textile and Weaving Structures
Batsford,1987
ISBN 0–7134-5645

Contemporary Crafts Museum & Gallery,
Portland, OR. 2004
Beyond Tradition: Contemporary Ply-Split Fiber Sculpture. (Exhibition catalogue)
ISBN 0-9728981-1-5

Dunsmore, Susi
Nepalese Textiles
British Museum Press. 1993
ISBN 0-7141-2510-5
Ply-Split Namlo.

Fraser, David.W
Ply-Split Baskets: Exploring Sculpture in Plain Oblique Twining.
Schiffer Publishing 2014
ISBN 978 0764342097
www.fraserfiber.com

Harvey, Virginia I.
Split-Ply Twining
Threads in Action, Monograph 1.1976
ISBN 0-916658-32-5

Haffenreffer Museum of Anthropology
Female costume of the Sarakatsani
Brown University1985
ISBN 0-91089-02-4.

Hatzimichali, Angeliki
The Greek Folk Costume
Benaki Museum. vols 1 & 2
Melissa Publishing House, 1979
Costume of the Sarakatsani

Hedges,Julie. Jessett, Sandy & Parry, Jennie
Basic Ply-Splitting.
Leaflet produced for the Braid Society
2003 & 2006. Available from the Braid Society.

Hedges, Julie
Ply-Split Braiding, An introduction to Designs in Single Course Oblique Twining.
Julie Hedges Books 2006 (1st Edition)
ISBN 13: 978-0-9554187-0-
2nd Edition. 2018
ISBN 13: 978-0-9554187-5-4

Hedges, Julie
Ply-Split Braiding, Further Techniques
Julie Hedges 2011
ISBN 13: 978-0-9554187-1-6

Hedges, Julie
Ply-Splitting in 3 Dimensions, An Introduction to making Vessels and Sculptural Forms
Julie Hedges Books 2013
ISBN 13: 978-0-9554187-2-3

Hedges, Julie
Ply-Split Braided Jewellery
Chokers and tubes. Roses and Crosses and Hexagon Bracelets.
Julie Hedges Books 2015
ISBN 13: 978-0-9554187-3-0

Hendrickson, Linda.
Great SCOT! A Beginner's Guide to Ply-Split Braids in Single Course Oblique Twining.
Hendrickson, 2000.

Hendrickson, Linda
How to Make Ply-Split Baskets, 2011.
www.lindahendrickson.com

Hendrickson, Linda.
How to Make Ply-Split Braids & Bands. 2014.
www.lindahendrickson.com

Norman, Ann & Ralph and **Parry, Jennie,** editors
Expanding the Girths
Published with the exhibition Expanding the Girths, traditional and contemporary ply–split braiding held in Bampton, Oxford, 2001
ISBN 0-9542420-0-9

Quick, Betsy D & Stein, Judith A
Ply-Split Camel Girths of West India
Pamphlet Series Volume 1, Number 7. 1982
Museum of Cultural History, UCLA Los Angeles

Spady, Robyn, editor
Braids, Bands and Beyond
Proceedings of the Third International Conference on Braiding: Braids 2016, Tacoma, USA,
Articles on Ply-Splitting by Julie Hedges, Linda Hendrickson and Barbara J.Walker.
www.braidsociety.com

Speiser, Noémi.
The Manual of Braiding. Basel, Switzerland, 1983.
Section on ply-splitting

Walker, Barbara J.
Ply-Splitting from Drawdowns
Interpreting Weave Structures in Ply-Split Braiding
BJW Publications, 2012.
ISBN: 978-0-9856293-0-4 2012
www.barbarajwalker.com

Ply-Split Braiding Articles

Andrews, Elizabeth
Influenced and inspired by the Sarakatsani people
The Journal of the Braid Society, 2016.
Strands, Issue 23

Collingwood, P and Parry, Jennie
A Miracle of Invention. Peter Collingwood discusses ply-split braiding with Jennie Parry,
Embroidery Vol 53 No.2 March 2002

Collingwood, P. Hedges J. Parry J. Speiser N.
Ply-Splitting Terminology, Strands,
The Journal of the Braid Society 2003.
Strands, Issue10

Collingwood, Peter.
"The Bowlor Hat."
Complex Weavers Journal, October 2005

Fraser, David.W
A family of radially symmetric, ply-split braided vessels. Shuttle, Spindle & Dyepot, XL, no. 3, Issue 159, Summer 2010
www.fraserfiber.com

Fraser, David.W
View from the shoulders of Thar masters: new spaces for ply-split braiding. Textile Society of America 2010, Symposium Proceedings.

Fraser, David W. "Asymmetry: Aesthetics and Politics of Ply-Split Braiding" (2012).
Textile Society of America Symposium Proceedings. Paper 684.

Fraser, David.W
Symmetric Vessels in Plain Oblique Twining
The Journal of the Braid Society, 2012.
Strands, Issue 19

French, Louise. "A Tisket, a Tasket, a Ply-Split Basket."
Handwoven, November/December 2011

French, Louise and Barbara J. Walker.
"Portable, Addictive: Ply-Splitting."
Weavezine. 30, November 2008.
www.weavezine.com/content/portable-addictive-ply-splitting

Hendrickson, Linda.
"Ply-Split Braiding."
Shuttle Spindle & Dyepot, Winter 2001/2002,

Hendrickson, Linda.
"Star Ornaments in Ply-Split Braiding."
Handwoven, Sept/Oct 2001

Hendrickson, Linda.
Ply-Split Garlic Basket. DVD.
www.lindahendrickson.com

Hedges Julie
Making Waves, an introduction to the technique of ply-split braiding, Strands,The Journal of the Braid Society 1998,Issue 5 and The World of Embroidery, May 2000 Vol 51 No.3

Hedges, Julie
Bands on the Costumes of the Sarakatsani,
The Journal of the Braid Society, 2004,
Strands, issue 11

Hedges, Julie
Looking for Ply-Split animal trappings in Rajasthan and Gujarat, North West India. The Journal for Weavers Spinners & Dyers, vol 214, June 2005.

Hedges, Julie
Some developments in Ply-Splitting, using three ply cords, The Journal of the Braid Society, 2010.
Strands, Issue 17

Parry, (Hedges) Julie
Basic Techniques: Making Cords,
Embroidery Autumn 1991 Vol 42 No 3

Walker, Barbara J.
"Learn Ply-Splitting with Two Summer Trivets."
Handwoven, March/ April 2011

Walker, Barbara J. "A Ply-Split Advancing Twill Belt." Complex Weavers Journal, Oct. 2012

Walker, Barbara J.
"Ply-Split Passementerie." The Journal of the Braid Society, Strands, Oct. 2013

Walker, Barbara J.
"Color Play: Designing Ply- Splitting Cords."
Complex Weavers Journal, Oct 2014

Walker, Barbara J.
"The Oh-So-Versatile Braid." The Journal of the Braid Society, Strands, Oct. 2015